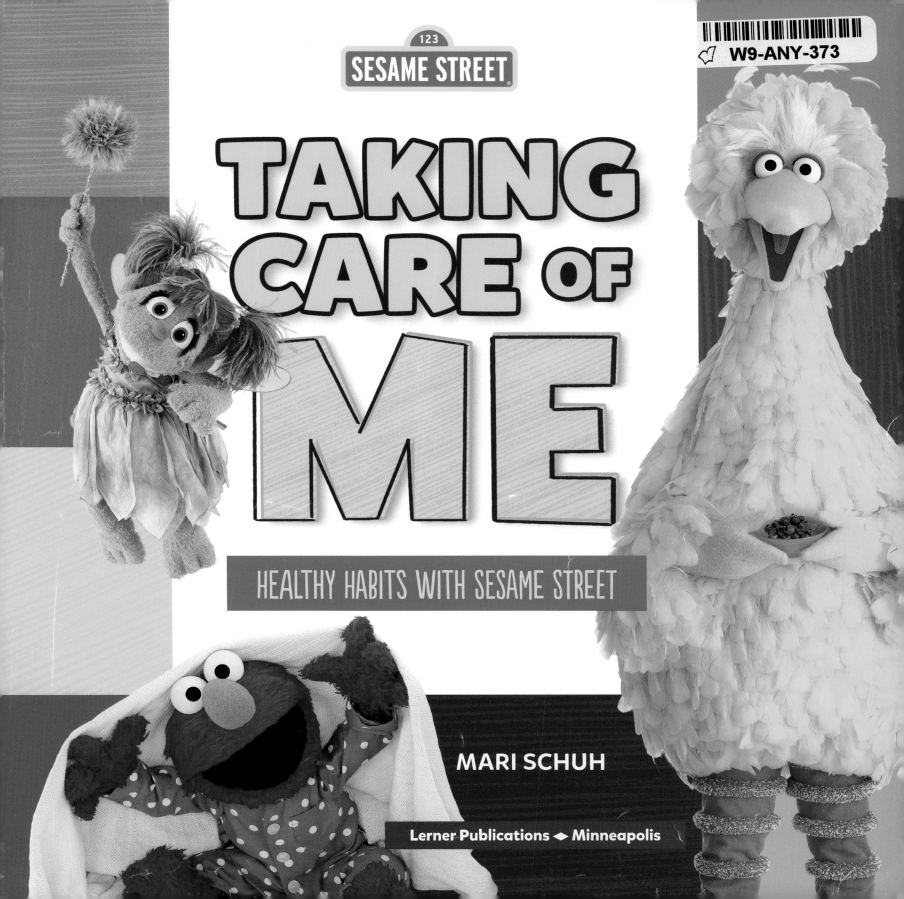

123
SESAME STREET®

TAKING CARE OF ME

HEALTHY HABITS WITH SESAME STREET

MARI SCHUH

Lerner Publications ◆ Minneapolis

Before you can help take care of your family, friends, or neighbors, it's important to learn how to take care of yourself. The whole furry, funny *Sesame Street* gang is here to show you how to keep healthy, from your body to your brain to your heart. Let's get started!

Sincerely,
the Editors at
Sesame Workshop

Table of Contents

Healthy Me

You can be a healthy kid.

Eat food that is good for you.
Run, jump, play.

Be healthy every day!

Eating good food keeps me happy and strong. And tall!

Being Healthy

Fruits and veggies are good for you. They make good snacks anytime.

Apples are good for me. Me eat apples anytime!

Some foods are treats. It's best to eat them only sometimes.

A birdseed cookie is a sometimes food.

7

Drinking water
every day is good
for your body.

When I drink lots of water, I am no longer thirsty. And I feel so adorable!

Scrub-a-dub-dub! Washing your hands gets rid of germs.

Elmo sings the ABCs. Then Elmo knows Elmo has washed long enough!

Wash your hands
after you use
the bathroom,
before you eat,
and after you
play outside.

When you are sick, keep your distance from other people.

Stand at least three trash cans away!

Sneeze into your elbow, a tissue, or a mask.

Wear a mask when you leave your home. That helps stop germs from spreading.

Moving makes
your body strong.

I dance!

Do things that
make you happy.

Play safely!
Wear a helmet when you ride a bike.

I wear sunscreen so I don't get sunburned!

Spend time
with the people
you love.

Being clean helps keep you healthy. Take a bath after a busy day.

Rubber Duckie makes bath time lots of fun!

Brush your teeth so they stay clean and strong. Floss too!

Brush
1 . . . 2 times
each day.
Ah, ah, ah!

Be sure to get enough sleep. Rest when you're tired.

Good night! Elmo loves you!

Make It a Habit

A habit is something you do often.

You brush your teeth every day. That's a good habit.

You can work with a friend to build good habits.

Healthy people have healthy habits.

You can too!

What are your healthy habits?

MY HEALTHY DAY

When it comes to health, every person—and monster!—has different needs. Talk to an adult about what is best for you. See how many of these healthy habits you can add to your day!

Eat fruits

Eat veggies

Drink water

Wash hands

Be active

Spend time with friends or family

Take a bath

Brush teeth and floss

Sleep

GLOSSARY

floss: to clean between your teeth with a piece of special thread

germ: a tiny living thing that causes sickness

habit: something that you do often

veggie: short for vegetable, a plant grown to be used as food

LEARN MORE

Arnéz, Lynda. *We Stay Healthy*. New York: Gareth Stevens, 2020.

Reinke, Beth Bence. *Healthy Eating Habits*. Minneapolis: Lerner Publications, 2019.

Schwartz, Heather E. *Cookie Monster's Foodie Truck: A Sesame Street Celebration of Food*. Minneapolis: Lerner Publications, 2020.

INDEX

PHOTO ACKNOWLEDGMENTS

Image credits: Africa Studio/Shutterstock.com, p. 4 (bottom); Jon Feingersh Photography Inc/DigitalVision/Getty Images, p. 4 (top); unguryanu/Shutterstock.com, p. 6; JPC-PROD/Shutterstock.com, p. 7 (top); Gordon Bell/Shutterstock.com, p. 7 (bottom); IllonajaIll/Shutterstock.com, p. 8; Oksana Kuzmina/Shutterstock.com, p. 11 (top); Daisy Daisy/Shutterstock.com, p. 11 (bottom); Prostock-studio/Shutterstock.com, p. 12; VaLiza/Shutterstock.com, p. 13; Denis Kuvaev/Shutterstock.com, p. 14; Cassiohabib/Shutterstock.com, p. 15 (top); Sergey Novikov/Shutterstock.com, p. 15 (bottom); Monkey Business Images/Shutterstock.com, pp. 16, 19; nd3000/Shutterstock.com, p. 18; Alexxndr/Shutterstock.com, p. 20 (top); PR Image Factory/Shutterstock.com, p. 20 (bottom); Casezy idea/Shutterstock.com, p. 22 (top); AAraujo/Shutterstock.com, p. 22 (bottom); wavebreakmedia/Shutterstock.com, p. 24 (top); Romrodphoto/Shutterstock.com, p. 24 (bottom); sabza/Shutterstock.com, p. 26 (top); masik0553/Shutterstock.com, p. 26 (bottom); Rawpixel.com/Shutterstock.com, p. 28.

For Autumn and Ella, healthy kids with healthy habits

Lerner Publications Company
An imprint of Lerner Publishing Group, Inc.
241 First Avenue North
Minneapolis, MN 55401 USA

For reading levels and more information, look up this title at www.lernerbooks.com.

Main body text set in Mikado. Typeface provided by HVD Fonts.

Editor: Andrea Nelson **Designer:** Laura Otto Rinne

Library of Congress Cataloging-in-Publication Data

Names: Schuh, Mari C., 1975- author.
Title: Taking care of me : healthy habits with Sesame Street / Mari Schuh.
Description: Minneapolis : Lerner Publications, [2021] | Audience: Ages 4–8 | Audience: Grades K-1 |
    Summary: "What is a habit? How do we make habits that are good for us? With help from their
    Sesame Street friends, young readers learn about the good choices they can make every day"
    – Provided by publisher.
Identifiers: LCCN 2020004998 (print) | LCCN 2020004999 (ebook) | ISBN 9781728403953 (library
    binding) | ISBN 9781728418612 (ebook)
Subjects: LCSH: Health—Juvenile literature. | Nutrition—Juvenile literature. | Health behavior—Juvenile
    literature.
Classification: LCC RA777 .S34 2021 (print) | LCC RA777 (ebook) | DDC 613—dc23

LC record available at https://lccn.loc.gov/2020004998
LC ebook record available at https://lccn.loc.gov/2020004999

Manufactured in the United States of America
1-48395-48909-6/18/2020